HIS FIRST YEAR THROUGH POETRY

THE TRUMP CHRONICLE

11/8/16
THROUGH
12/9/17

IRVIN R. BROOKSTEIN
AKA RAYRAY

Design by Deborah Perdue, Illumination Graphics
Illustration by Tara Thelen
Original Sketch by Terry Ann Pertler
Author photos by Lindsey Renstrom,
Sweet Peas Photography

Interior photos courtesy of http://creativecommons.org/
licenses/by/2.0/
PhotosforClass.com
and DepositPhotos.com

ISBN 978-0-692-05605-9

ACKNOWLEDGMENTS

About a year ago, as I was putting the finishing touches on my first book of poetry, *Rays of Light*, I had an idea.

For at least a year prior, I had been battling a political fight almost everyday, with family members, close friends and almost everyone I encountered in Denver, over the Trump campaign. I heard the drone everyday on CNN, MSNBC, and the media, how horrible this man was and that only an idiot and a racist could support his campaign.

There were very few allies and an army of enemies. Thankfully, I had one ally, my Mom, and one cable TV station, FOX News.

I gave up on reading any newspapers due to the heavy slant against this brave soul who was up against the establishment of Democrats and Republicans. He had his own voice and virtually no support anywhere. I started to see that this was not going to be pretty. Nothing I could say, Nothing I could think mattered. My voice was being squelched and my family was at odds over this political divide.

As Donald Trump started to gain momentum, I stuck by Mom and FOX News because the assault against his presidency was becoming more extreme, with no place to hide and no forum to express support for this man.

I, like many people, kept my mouth shut and observed in silence. It didn't seem worth getting into a political debate, because the opposition was, and still is, utterly immovable in their position, that this man is below the worst form of dirt and a curse against humanity. As he started to plow through every political opponent, it started to become clear that he was going to get the nomination against all odds.

Wow, a NY real estate magnate and TV star running for President! The focus was..would he get enough delegates. Yada yada yada. Everyone was wrong and he prevailed to be on the ballot on 11/8/16. So I had an idea to be a voice. Little 'ole RayRay with no real political savvy, no political debate experience, no in depth understanding of the political games and little grasp of the issues at hand. But I was convinced I was going to be a voice. Having a voice is our right and duty as Americans. Otherwise we lose and will be crushed.

However, what I do have is a skill. Wow, that sounds like Liam Neeson in "Taken." That skill is to put ideas into rhythm and rhyme expressed through poems.

If you asked me to express it through back and forth communication, I would probably get tongue tied and fail miserably in getting my points across. But through poems, I can do well.

A year ago, we probably approached the most important day in the modern political history of the United States of America, 11/8/16, Election Day. As the evening progressed, reality started to sink in, that the greatest upset in political history was about to occur ~ Donald

Trump was going to be elected the 45th president of the United States of America.

At that moment, I decided I wanted to chronicle the first year of his presidency through poetry. I have put forth 47 poems, starting on Election Day and progressing through the first year, and what a year it has been!

In this chronological anthology, there are no essays, no blogs, no detailed analysis, no numbered or lettered lists detailing the reasons for things, one way or the other, just poetry, based on emotion and expressions of the heart to warm the souls of millions of silent supporters that changed the course of modern political history. This work is for you ~ one man's voice for you!

Each day provided ample material as you may know.

As I write this acknowledgment on 10/24/17 just a few short weeks from the anniversary of this Election Day surprise, only another massacre or confrontation with North Korea, would necessitate another poem or two. So onward to get this published in a timely fashion.

I want to thank my mother Stella; Bill Wilson of Pompano Beach, FL; Bob Carreiro of the Villages, FL; Jeffrey W. Szekely of Rockville, MD; Howie Waldman of Hicksville, NY; Marie Bianco Blair of Lincoln, NE; Patti Casciola Stern of Laguna Hills, CA; and Terry Ann Pertler of Douglas, WY for their help and inspiration to create the poems, graphics and foreword for this chronicle. I hope you enjoy it.

Love with special regards,
Irvin R. Brookstein
AKA RayRay

FOREWORD

Irvin R. Brookstein's second book of poetry, *The Trump Chronicle* is a phenomenal display of poetic prowess and versatility. Here, the author has designed a bridge, a political intervention if you may. RayRay writes to calm the savage fury, not only with the purpose of soothing, but also to reflect upon this abysmal emotional divide that has separated families, even torn apart longtime friendships, to quell this aura that permeates our country today. RayRay's poetry is a mirror to this chaotic world, his words and rhyme providing the moving force to "bridge" this ugly divide that continues to rear its head along every moral, religious and political line. With his powerful pen, RayRay provides the inspiration and motivation to spur each and every one of us to coexist, to truly understand one another and to rid this world of hatred.

No one will deny the import and impact of social media that was generated during this campaign and in the successive days of Donald Trump's Presidency. Having a very strong following on social media himself, his readers coming from all walks of life, even spanning the globe, RayRay's fans never hesitate to express what RayRay's poetry, especially what this book of poetry, means to them.

Fueled by Social Media, I would like to share some of the commentary that represents a cross section of the ideologies and geographic diversity that form our country in the passages below.

Left, Right, Misogyny, Radical Islam, America First, our economy, their economy, everyone else first This chronology of poems beautifully details Donald Trump's first year in office in such honest, humorous and wonderfully sarcastic detail. Ray's ability to take our current events and put them into words has certainly raised the bar for other poets and hopefully will help others understand with brutal honesty the reality of our country's situation.

The chasm that has formed and that has divided our country seems to grow wider and more radical by the day. As a former US ARMY Captain, Paratrooper and Pilot-in- command UH-1H, I know and recognize the urgency and absolute necessity of keeping our country and our citizens safe from foreign interests. There are so many individuals from many different countries and belief systems who only have one goal, and that is to kill Americans because of what we believe in, and what we stand for.

Our borders, security and our nation's economy should be our leader's first and most important priority. Bowing to and allowing other countries and factions within our own country to manipulate us is disgraceful and dishonors every man or woman who has served or given their life for this great nation.

In order for our country to thrive and survive, we must protect our people and our economy. As a disabled veteran, I am saddened to see such divisiveness over such ideals as safety and economic growth. To see billions and billions of dollars given to foreign terrorists sponsoring nations is a travesty at best, while our own country has so many internal issues and external threats.

Our great nation needs to come together during these difficult times. As a soldier who stood on that wall, sworn to protect and defend our constitution against enemies foreign and domestic, I am deeply saddened at the lack of common sense that seems to be so pervasive.

If a soldier is asked what he prays for most of all, they will say peace, safety and economic security for their family and their country.

God bless America,
William W. Wilson, Jr.
Pompano Beach, Florida

In January 2017, Donald Trump was sworn in as our 45th President, the first ever without any political or military experience. An outsider! A man of great wealth and success, clearly a man with a mind and agenda of his own.

Immediately following this President's election, our institutions of higher learning broke out in hives. Students required counseling, safe spaces and special privileges. Political correctness replaced free speech. A wave of which washed over America, as our most anti-PC President began to make his mark. Cultural appropriation became a national preoccupation. It brought forth one of my favorite 2017 sayings, "When everything is an outrage, nothing is!" Students demonstrated, rioted and in some cases burned the place down. If they felt the voice that was scheduled to speak was not in sync with their voice they demanded that that speaker be silenced.

The free press proved to be a misnomer and a shill for the progressive agenda. To this President Trump spent much time lambasting the "Crooked Press," and the "Fake News." Celebrities and D.C. insulted us with sexual harassment and worse scandals while they continued to lecture us about the right betraying true American values by electing President Trump. All of this raging while preoccupying us with Monumentgate and ridiculous events such as ESPN pulling an Asian American announcer whose last name is Lee because of the confederate general hysteria. And so many senseless crimes were committed by illegal interlopers protected by the Sanctuary State status. To Wall or not to Wall continued to be the question. Along with the myriad of new gender identities, and the ever present, concept, how do we self-identify?

It's been a truly unprecedented year in the Upside Down.

Because of this, and because I love Ray's style and insights, I enthusiastically invite you to travel the "Year of Trump" through an exciting 12 months of Ray's chronicling the first of eight years of Donald Trump's Presidency.

Patti Casciola Stern
Laguna Hills, California

Ray's book of poems is a compelling compilation of the first year of President Trump's term in office. It is not only very worthwhile, but I would venture to say an exceptional collection of poems in a world that has not witnessed a first term President of such magnitude.

I live 12 miles from the White House in Maryland and have followed politics since I was 10 years old. Having read many books on the body politic over a lifetime, I can safely say that Ray has captured the essence of our 45th President in verse.

Ray truly understands, because he possesses keen insight in the political, social, and economic arena. He delves into the thought process of President Trump and is able to convey this, appealing to the feelings of the American public.

I have never experienced such a unique, timely representation of the first year of a President and to be able to put it in poetic form.

Quite frankly, it is remarkable and beyond the pale.

Jeffrey W. Szekely
Rockville, Maryland

Ray Brookstein, captures in his prose, the political scene from the time that then candidate Trump announced to the American people that he was going to "Make America Great Again." He shows the opposition's views as fear and distrust. His poetry helps to tell the truth after the election of President Trump and the changes he has in mind to keep that promise to America. The "left" is in shock that their candidate "lost mentality" has taken to violence and unprovoked verbal attacks on the President.

Ray's poetry perfectly tells the story in a sequence from the beginning to the present of the real life thoughts of a "Right" minded citizen in a world of jumbled chaos.

Howie Waldman
Hicksville, New York

As you can readily see from the commentary above, it is agreed that RayRay's unique style of poetry, using his tongue-in-cheek humor, his rhythm and rhyme, appeals to all readers not only across the political arena, but a geographical one as well. You will surely see that through his words, RayRay has singlehandedly opened the lines of discourse across America to a better understanding of our 45th President and the work that he is doing during his first year in the White House.

I now invite you to embark upon this journey and to cross that "bridge" to the understanding, insight and reflection that RayRay provides.

Marie Bianco Blair
Lecturer in Spanish
University of Nebraska
Lincoln, Nebraska

CONTENTS

Election Night 2016

Blue States were fading
All over the map
Polls told the story
Cable stations react

They expected a landslide
From West to the East
Middle America voted
Now poised for a feast

Flip-flopping logic
It must be a trick
Recount all those ballots
They couldn't resist

Behold the election
Shocking with awe
Trump is victorious
The Left never foresaw

The Electoral College
Took them to school
Democracy preserved
Constitutionally cool

Hillary's fireworks
Became duds on the street
Democrats wailing
Finally tasting defeat

Campuses scramble
To find a safe space
Congress upheavals
All over the place

The die has been cast
Conservatives glee
Perhaps God intervened
So we dropped to our knee

So now time will tell
Our history's tale
We pray for our President
That peace will prevail

Written by RayRay 11/9/16

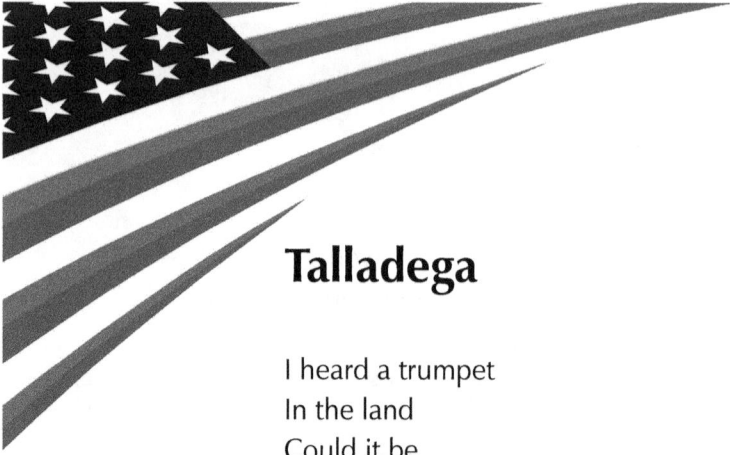

Talladega

I heard a trumpet
In the land
Could it be
A Bama band?

A shofar shrill
A clarion call
Perhaps that sound
Was good for all

To their proud parents
Who watched with glee
Their children
Making history

Without disgust
Without the hate
So politicized
At such a rate

It cud be your child
Who was in a play
That filled your pride
Upon the stage

Some did not approve
And said their piece
In every moment
A chance to teach

Sometimes it's best
To button up
Bite our tongues
When times get tough

Heed the sound
That children hear
That sound of love
Once in our ear

But for a day
To put aside
An inauguration
Still filled with pride

Written by RayRay 1/19/17

Ground Zero

It didn't take long
As they say
With tempers hot
On marching day

Grab ur sign
Stating facts
Don't you love
Our pussy hats?

We don't care
If you agree
We won't get down
Upon our knee

We hate you Trump
We hate that voice
Can't wait to change
Electoral choice

Every minute
Of every day
Every hour
In every way

We'll kick some butt
In the street
Vomiting
Each time you tweet

Someone wake me
From my despair
Nightmarish visions
Of orange hair

So just be ready
On the spot
We will hit u with
Our best left shot

So be on guard
You'll pay a price
Should you confirm
A Jew named Christ

Written by RayRay 1/22/17

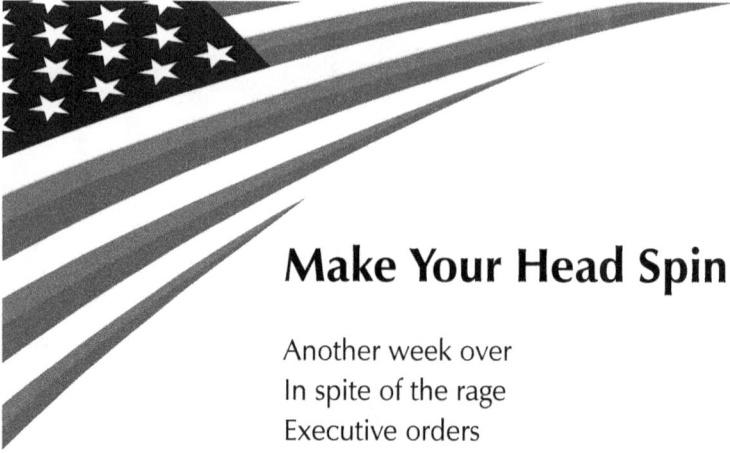

Make Your Head Spin

Another week over
In spite of the rage
Executive orders
Dry ink on the page

He met with the unions
Theresa May too
With a stature of Churchill
Enjoying the view

Finish the pipelines
In the U S of A
While Native Americans
Expressed their dismay

Madonna and Ashley
Raising their voice
Pro Lifers marching
For alternative choice

97% of scientists
Insist temperatures rise
But not of the science
Which constitutes life

Alternative facts
Of alternative views
Without viewing options
All of us lose

Nieto and Putin
Waiting on deck
Cabinet confirms
Supreme Court is next

So buckle your seat belt
For a furious week
Nothing comes easy
To get what you seek

Written by RayRay 1/28/17

And the Ban Plays On

He put his foot down
Just like he had said
Some feel outright betrayal
When constitutionally read

Iran flexed its muscles
To no one's surprise
For within every action
Its opposite lies

Just like a tuning fork
Which resonates sound
Can only reach balance
When it slows itself down

He knew taking action
Would set off alarms
Awake from a slumber
Of significant times

So the Ban has begun
And protests abound
I noted no casualties
At least.. none could be found

Written by RayRay 1/28/17

ICBM

You may be a hawk
Or you may be a dove
But Iranian missiles
Are more than a shove

It's not wise to provoke
In aggressive detail
It's more than just testing
It's peace that could fail

It didn't take long
For this man voted in
To put them on notice
Their thinking won't win

Peace is our purpose
But sometimes it takes
A fervent response
When our freedom's at stake

It's never good timing
When dealing with this
Testing our mettle
But we have to resist

Perhaps economic
Diplomatically framed
But pushing the button
We have to restrain

So take a deep breath
And softly exhale
Trust that our leadership
Heads will prevail

Written by RayRay 2/1/17

The Lull Before the Storm

Like prize fighters poised
To ready the fight
Sides lining up
As to whom's side is right

If ever an issue
Has come into view
Supreme courting Justice
For a generation or two

From every direction
Issues appear
From all sides a battle
Overwhelming clear

When power is shifted
They forge the path
Pitting frayed moral judgement
Against mission at hand

Promises made
Promises kept
Hope vision is clear
That we all can accept

Many are feeling
A deepening mess
Perhaps Super Bowl Sunday
Will relieve some distress

Written by RayRay 2/1/17

The Battle Begins

The sabers are sharpened
The lawyers are swift
Orally arguing
Whether borders exist

Some see the matter
As simple and sane
Can we choose who comes in
On the refugee train?

While no one disputes
The American dreams
Loving Lady Liberty
And all what that means

Our times are quite different
Real threats abound
Do we abandon our sovereignty
Due to loudness of sound?

The lawyers will argue
The judges will test
Constitutional issues
Neutral from the protests

We voted them in
Appointed them too
Americans live by the outcome
In spite of our view

Some vowed they would leave us
Depends on who wins
I'm not sure that happened
One-way tickets turned in

We live in a country
Where diversity thrives
With our one Constitution
Guiding our lives

So before we go crazy
For sanity's sake
Let the process unfold
Our country's at stake

Written by RayRay 2/6/17

The Devos Wears Prada

The nuclear option
Was there on the spot
Confirming Devos
Ready or not

They jumped and they hissed
Petitioned and prayed
But educationally speaking
We all got Amway'd

Whether public or private
Or Chartered Home Schooled
We wish that our children
Become billionaires too

Raising objections
When up for a job
Trust in 100 Senators
With the VP on top

We gave him the safe
Along with the keys
Educating our children
With their I E P's

Many shaking their heads
And all at a loss
That another Trump card
Has kept Betsy Devos

Written by RayRay 2/7/17

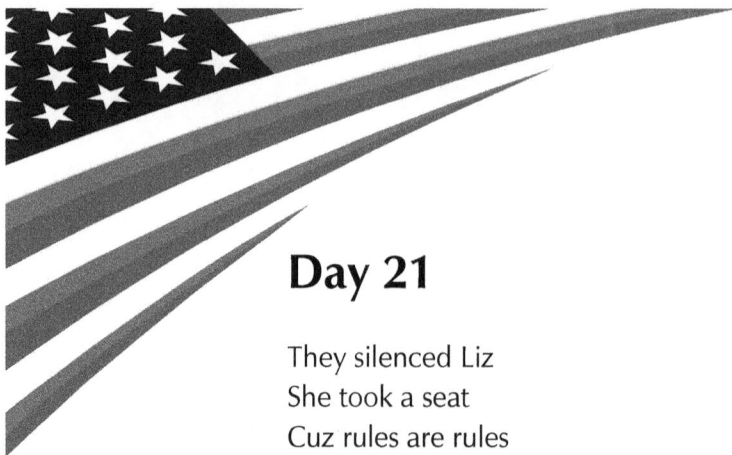

Day 21

They silenced Liz
She took a seat
Cuz rules are rules
Short and sweet

The man she dissed
All about
Sessions's in
So stomp and pout

They got the word
From the court
Upheld the stay
So time is bought

Previous precedent
Put aside
So fill the lines
While his hands are tied

So up the ladder
And place your bet
Supreme Court's next
Put to the test

Two steps forward
One step back
Return to your corners
To plan the attack

Written by RayRay 2/10/17

First Trimester

Events come so swiftly
Can't catch your own breath
She visits a grade school
To find signs marked for death

No one could fashion
The signs at the mall
Nordstrom was playing
Political hardball

Why should it matter
If you're Red or you're Blue
Protecting one's daughter
Any father would do

Shinzo would visit
Then heading due south
Golfing with Donald
Then sushi by mouth

Confirming Tom Price
To repeal and replace
For Obamacare lovers
A spit in the face

ICE is on fire
Executive orders go cold
Some say this is progress
But I'll let it unfold

While it's only 3 months
Since the ballots were cast
You can bet your last dollar
There are millions aghast

Written by RayRay 2/11/17

Valentine's Day Massacre

The noose always tightens
When trust is at risk
Flynn takes a bullet
Then resigns and desists

One month and counting
Stirring the soup
Leaks in the water
Boils intelligence groups

National Security
Put to the ropes
North Korea launches
Russian spies off the coast

It seems like a novel
Except that it's real
It might be a best seller
When the theme is revealed

There are seldom light moments
So let me be frank
Trudeau needs our border
Or NHL ratings might tank

Mnuchin's confirmed
As the treasury vents
Venezuelan drug lords
Stealing dollars and cents

So hang on to your hats
The ride's getting rough
Opposition on the warpath
Exploiting this stuff

Written by RayRay 2/14/17

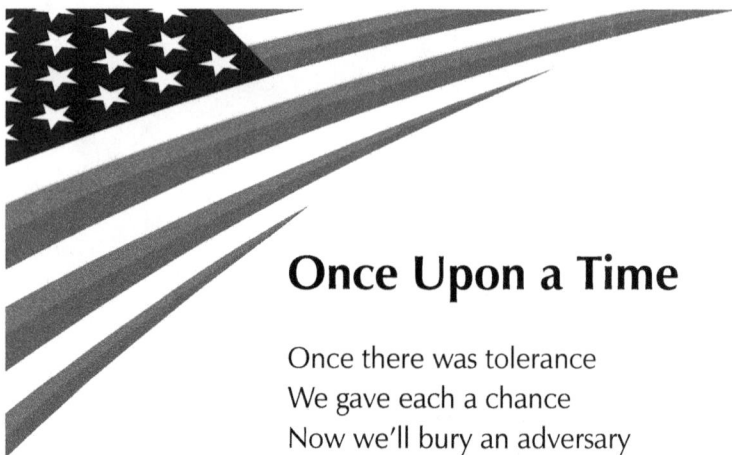

Once Upon a Time

Once there was tolerance
We gave each a chance
Now we'll bury an adversary
Because of their stance

Once there was justice
Now just a rope
Guilt from a mob
While proof is a joke

Once there was freedom
To say what you felt
Now watch your own back
And prepare for a welt

Once there was a country
For me and for you
Now it's divided
Broken in two

Once there was pride
And bounce in our step
Now there is violence
From right and the left

Once we were patriots
With similar thoughts
Now an internal battle
Is about to be fought

Once there was brotherhood
Sisterhood too
Now we are colorblind
It's either Red or it's Blue

Once there were symbols
Appealing for peace
Where has the love gone?
With hate on the increase

It's time to take stock
Give the process a chance
Change is uncomfortable
A new step in the dance

Believe in democracy
It's not on the run
It's still solidly here
Good things still to come

Have a positive outlook
It works ever so well
It's time that our oceans
Have a more positive swell

Written by RayRay 2/16/17

The Press Conference

He didn't hold back
Not quite tactful redress
He poked and he prodded
And skewered the Press

While Bibi departed
And doing his job
He showed the Prime Minister
How to make shish kebob

He answered all questions
Some felt he abused
Not pleased that he mentioned
They were trolling fake news

The pundits reported
Chaos and dread
So he stepped to the podium
And condemned what they said

If you're looking for change
To the man at the mic
Then believe the Tooth Fairy
Will deliver your bike

We believe in free press
That's unquestionably true
For the voice of the people
Should always shine through

But you can take to the bank
How press conferences will go
When you deal with this President
It's all part of the show

Written by RayRay 2/17/17

The Roast

They invited him
But he won't go
Be in the crosshairs
To the flamers throw

He faces fire
Everyday
He won't give in
To be their prey

They'll put a target
On his head
To make sure that
Their lion's fed

While most roasts
Are for comedy
Where you bite your tongue
And take the heat

This one comes
At such a time
Frankly it's his choice
To decline

These correspondents
May stomp and pout
That the one they sought
Has slithered out

But it's not so bad
I have no doubt
Let them enjoy
Their dinner out

But this time
The tradition bent
The sitting duck
Will not relent

So lick your chops
To your dismay
This time this one
Got away

Written by RayRay 2/25/17

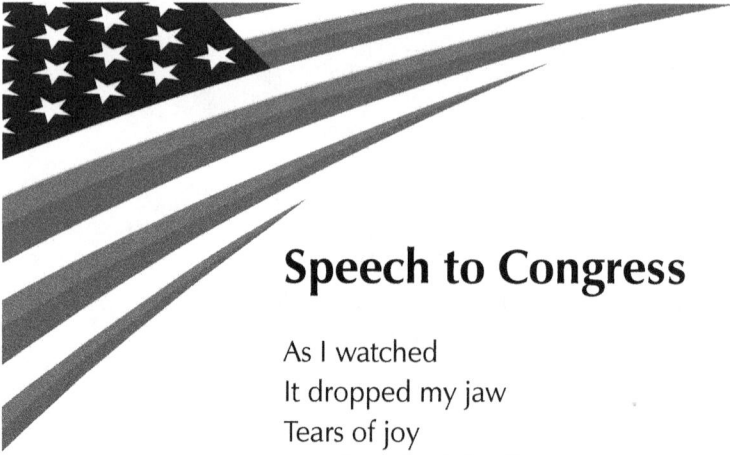

Speech to Congress

As I watched
It dropped my jaw
Tears of joy
Just drenched the floor

It's not like I hadn't
Heard before
Similar words
He would implore

This man takes it
On the chin
Impervious to pain
Poised to win

I hoped this time
He could captivate
Even those
Intent on hate

Mrs. Owens
Tore my heart
When she looked above
I fell apart

That one moment
Galvanized
A country needing
That cleansing cry

Boldly speaking
From his heart
Uniting us for
A brand new start

What struck me most
Through my tears
Was how far we've come
In 250 years

Last night marked
A brand new day
An American President
I'm proud to say

I believe in him
Though many laugh
I hoped he touched
The other half

Written by RayRay 3/1/17

Y R Taps

It's out in the light
How dark it's become
Where ever you turn
We're under a thumb

We should not be surprised
It's been going on for years
From M to James Bond
And all of their peers

Internet companies
Cell carriers too
Even your TV
Is listening to you

There's no place to hide
Appalachia too
They're tracking your movements
To moonshine and brew

Every American's
Very smart phone
Even a dumb one
Won't leave u alone

This is America
While it may be absurd
Whether we like it or not
They record every word

We hope they decipher
The good from the bad
The right from the wrong
The mad from the glad

So stay off of your phone
TV or PC
Get to the beach
Or a mountain top peak

Then whisper your message
Right into an ear
Out in the open
Where no one can hear

If that doesn't work
Then all u can say
Privacy's history
In the U S of A

Written by RayRay 3/9/17

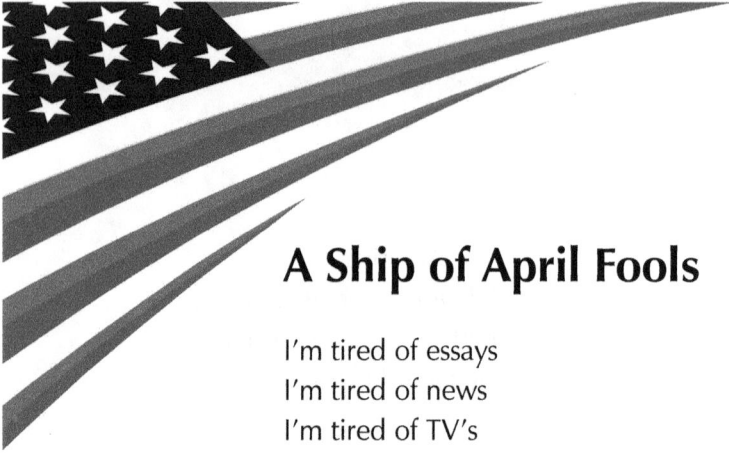

A Ship of April Fools

I'm tired of essays
I'm tired of news
I'm tired of TV's
Media abuse

I'm tired of Obama
He had his chance
I'm tired of Hillary
And her circumstance

I'm tired of Russia
I'm tired of leaks
No matter what he does
The opposition freaks

But the worst of it
Is how I feel
When family and friends
Attack with zeal

I thought that Democracy
Gives us choice
But they squelch our right
Impinge our voice

Arrogance
Will never work
Is there intelligence
Within a jerk?

The time has come
We stood up tall
Our strength is what
Will make them stall

Tolerance
Is what they preach
Forgetting blindly
What they teach

When I lose
It won't take long
To figure out
Just what went wrong

Life is tough
When it goes awry
We grit our teeth
And question why

If I want answers
To my disgust
In a shiny mirror
Is what I trust

Written by RayRay 4/1/17

The Scale of Justice

We've learned that our Justice
Will supposedly be
Blind as a bat
But I've heard that they see

The stakes are so high
The lines have been drawn
A tip of the scale
That won't take very long

The Right stifled Garland
And they're still quite annoyed
The sighs and the gasping
Over the seat that is void

The Progressive – like leaning
Is so ever at risk
They never imagined
It could end up like this

The tide has just risen
With anticipation
Drop the nuclear option
Without radiation

So gather your guns
For a Supreme Courting duel
Libs may have to live life
Under Conservative rule

The fear that will grow
With all hair turning grey
"Only in America"™
Just like Don King would say

Written by RayRay 4/2/17

Fly the Friendly Skies

Another week is over
Our leader took a stand
When they gas our precious children
A response that it demands

The tomahawks got launched
A message clearly sent
The world will take a pause
To interpret what it meant

North Korea threatens
Ignoring us this week
Beware the 38th Parallel
Will be disappearing in a blink

And what of Mother Russia
Acting like a dinosaur
Thinking they can devour
T-Rex at their front door

While back at home we're happy
That Gorsuch got confirmed
Scalia clapping in his grave
As the Democrats got spurned

When u consider summer travel
It may be rather wise
To fly American or Southwest
Not United's friendly skies

Written by RayRay 4/11/17

The Seven Seas

Both sides square off
They're poised for a fight
Gathering criticism
From Left and the Right

This isn't a prize fight
Nor W W E
Not a pay-per-view showcase
On Cable TV

We're watching each move
Of how they behave
I guarantee my father
Is astir in his grave

I hope we are listening
To the bottom line call
When you threaten America
It threatens us all

Many may question
The wisdom of this
Every country's affected
Not a time to desist

When you consider alternatives
And the issue at hand
Others fall short
Of the one this demands

We fight for equality
We fight for latrines
Animal cruelty
And what Climate Change means

But survival of freedom
Is the only true fight
One resounding purpose
Not who's Left or who's Right

Though it might be a dare
Though it might be a bluff
We must gather our arsenal
When the seas get this rough

Written by RayRay 4/20/17

Slip Sliding Away

It's slipping away
In front of our eyes
The end of free speech
So don't act so surprised

What have we wrought
Inside of our child
We thought tolerance lives
Instead it's gone wild

We thought American campuses
Were places to learn
Explore one's future career
Not set fires to burn

We cannot sit idly
It's no time to hush
Put hands in our pockets
And say what's the rush

Don't wear your red hat
Don't show your true face
The wave that's forthcoming
No greater disgrace

Instead we take shelter
We're lying in wait
Better grab constitutions
Before it's too late

The elders got wiser
While the youngins got dumb
We softened their instincts
They avoided our thumb

So now we behold
The generation called Z
While the Boomers are vanishing
Like you and like me

What kind of legacy
What have we left
Just a slippery slope
And a freedomly theft

Written by RayRay 4/27/17

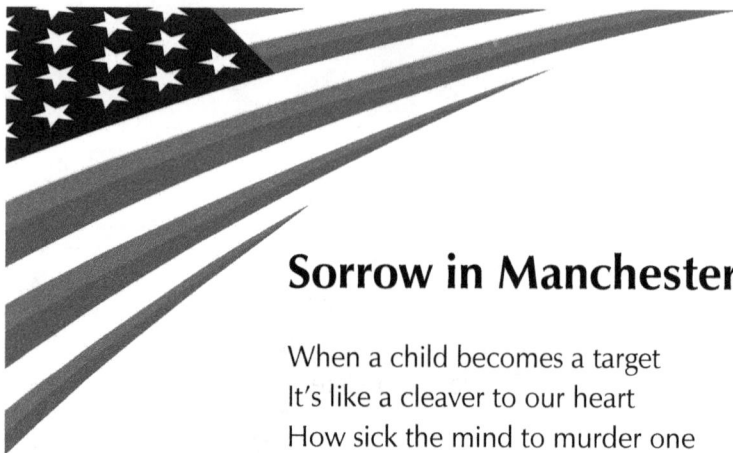

Sorrow in Manchester

When a child becomes a target
It's like a cleaver to our heart
How sick the mind to murder one
And be rewarded for their part

A future done forever
The light of someone's life
The darkness of the moment
Endless grief consuming strife

Our precious little treasures
Become our precious teens
Maturing into an adult
Await their family dreams

Their safety is our burden
We have to take a stand
Do whatever must be done
Cuz it's gotten out of hand

Our children are the future
Every single one
Fighting existential threats
The time to act has come

Regardless of your party
It's not a time to blame
It's time we stand together
Let no parent face this pain

If it takes a bow and arrow
Or a sharpened bayonet
We have to fight them at their source
Cuz no other choice is left

Written by RayRay 5/23/17

American Pastime

What started with practice
To cover the base
Was shattered by gunfire
Such a bloody disgrace

Some said they deserved it
How callous and mean
Our Congressmen targeted
Is completely obscene

I lived through the madness
Of assassins crosshairs
Brothers Johnny and Robert
MLK and despair

I know there's desperation
When life has its pain
But to see Democracy's progress
Go completely insane

They wanted to savor
The green of the turf
Shag a few flys
And slide in the earth

Just live a life freely
Safely and rich
With bat, glove and baseballs
And whacking that pitch

It's time we remember
It's not for fortune nor fame
Just serving their country
And the love of the game

Written by RayRay 6/21/17

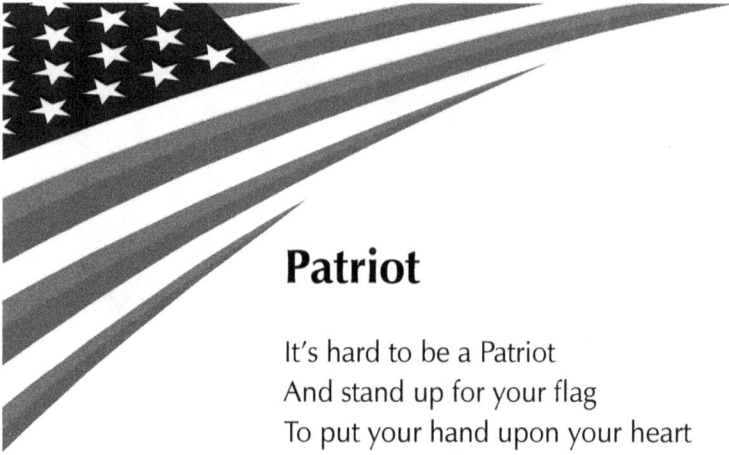

Patriot

It's hard to be a Patriot
And stand up for your flag
To put your hand upon your heart
When others think it's sad

It's hard to be a Patriot
To feel that unity
To know that call for freedom
To some a travesty

It's hard to be a Patriot
To know the love of home
To love that hallowed piece of ground
While others throw a stone

The causes will confuse us
So trust what's in your heart
The answer stretches everyone
When seams get pulled apart

The meaning of a Patriot
Will stand the test of time
Every human everywhere
Will struggle to define

So draw your own conclusion
Wrangle with the thought
It's time we all address the word
For the meaning we have sought

To call yourself a Patriot
Is not a dirty word
To believe it might be otherwise
Is clearly quite absurd

Written by RayRay 7/4/17

Don't Be Fooled

It may feel like it's crumbling
But not in the core
The dead leaves are falling
And may litter the floor

You may think you're winning
By knocking him down
But one doesn't elevate
When you tarnish the crown

You may think that you're reaching
The truth of the Left
The mirage they believe in
Amounts to felonious theft

The heart of this leader
Has been battered before
The death of his brother
Made a Jedi restore

The truth of the matter
Is the depth of support
We may not be as vocal
Or show destructive retort

From the heart of this nation
There's a clamoring call
Protecting our rights
And justice for all

His path wasn't chosen
He answered the bell
He values our freedom
Our grandchildren will spell

So before celebrating
And raising your fists
60 million Americans
Will peacefully resist

Although he is characterized
As sly as a fox
We show our approval
In a balloted box

Written by RayRay 7/21/17

Baby Boomer Amends

It's been about 50 years
Since the offensive named TET
But the only offense
Was never honoring these Vets

We protested this war
One never declared
50,000 daughters and sons
Their deathly burden to bare

Be careful to criticize
Those that dodged and deferred
Some forget it was commonplace
To hide in the herd

We mourned the soldiers
Who never came back
Yet abandoned survivors
When they undid their pack

Some without limbs
Bodies abused
Chemically altered
Agent Orange infused

The courageous came home
To a shameful disgrace
Some were offered a job
But most.. spat in the face

We worry more about climate
And fresh water to keep
Than finding a home
For a Vet on the street

These brothers of war
Continued the fight
Desert Storm Iraqi freedom
With no end in sight

Haunted by memories
Mentally and physically harmed
Suicide's rampant
Yet no one's alarmed

It's never too late
Helping those in despair
It takes more than a pill
Or a psychiatrist's chair

Let's start with a hug
For love that was lost
Fix the VA
No matter the cost

It's time we pay homage
To the last of these men
And the irony of it all
Is that they'd gladly do it again

Written by RayRay 8/6/17

Rewriting History

The world has gone mad
It's so simple to see
Because we don't like it
We will erase history?

Thinking they're cleansing
Rewriting it themselves
Might as well burn a book
Right there on the shelf

Reminds me of Adolph
Jews piled in a hole
Erasing their history
So truth can't be told

To those that repeat this
A lesson not learned
Pull down a monument
A Confederate flag you will burn

The Washington Monument
Demolition you'll see
Because tree huggers got angry
Because George cut a tree

But of course when it suits them
They'll connect their own dots
Compare Donald to Hitler
Whether truthful or not

Thinking this strategy
Will pay off in the end
But it's they that are fascist
Tho they'd like to pretend

We may not be proud
Of deeds we have done
There's no one alive
Who hasn't done wrong

But burying history
Will not fool a soul
We pray we survive this
So our children will know

That history teaches us
The good and the bad
Let them judge for themselves
Not on some vacated pad

Written by RayRay 9/1/17

Inheriting History

The lessons of history
Should not be ignored
Should not be forgotten
And mindfully stored

The division is hard
Separation is raw
The blood of the battles
Erupts in our craw

It could be as simple
As an argument we had
Just a moment ago
Or events a hundred years past

It's true when we live them
It's our history
But before we were born
I'm sure you'll agree

That history is inherited
All over the world
Children from everywhere
It's all that they've heard

It's not our experience
We can claim as our own
It's the feelings we hold
As we have grown

It colors the present
Though we weren't the cause
Shame, guilt or elation
We gotta take pause

While we condemn
The ills of the past
The truth is it's gone
The die has been cast

All we can do
Is live a new day
Breathe in fresh air
And make our own history today

Written by RayRay 8/2/17

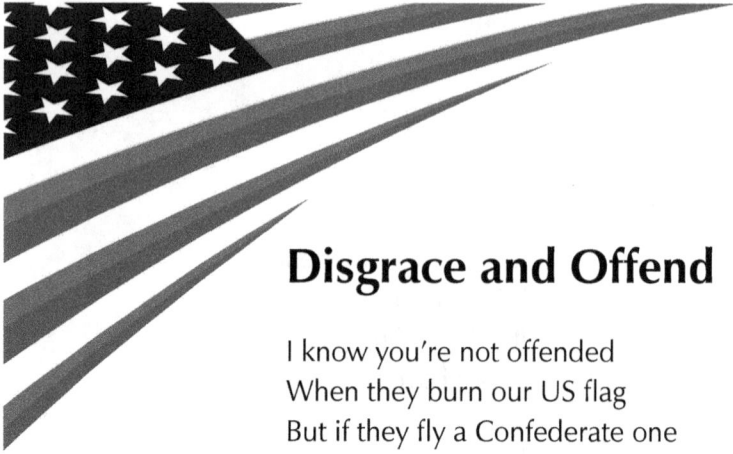

Disgrace and Offend

I know you're not offended
When they burn our US flag
But if they fly a Confederate one
I suspect you'll be steaming mad

I doubt you'll be offended
When they behead and brutally stab
But you'll protect sanctuary criminals
In point of fact . . . be glad

You're not at all offended
When they abort an unborn child
But you'll rebuild transgender bathrooms
To urinate in style

You're clearly not offended
When they ambush sitting cops
But corralling gangs of felons
Makes you pissy poop and plotz

You proved you're not offended
When an obstructing Congress stalls
But God forbid they fortify
A porous Southern Wall

It offended your Left Wing morals
When the electoral vote came down
Trump was elected President
Foiling Hillary Clinton's crown

So bring on 2020
When re-election day is through
So we can relish 4 more years
Of deplorables offending you

Written by RayRay 8/13/17

Sweet Dreams

This may surprise you
When we're on the Right
Our lives are so peaceful
We sleep thru the night

You may think that we're idiots
But It won't phase us at all
The louder you scream
On deafer ears it will fall

You try to enrage us
By raising your fist
Keep stomping your feet
While we let your chaos persist

You're angry and spiteful
Defiantly speak
Your protest is grotesque
Obvious kinks in your link

You don't like our religions
You don't like that we pray
You forgot please and thank you
You just tossed it away

You just can not fathom
The way which we think
Insist that the climate
Puts our earth on the brink

You don't like our rifles
Our trucks or RVs
The beers which we drink
Or what we watch on TV

Everything appalls you
We are an evil disgrace
You won't let us speak on a campus
While you need a safe space

It's you who doesn't get
What this is about
Try preserving America
And not tossing it out

Your arrogance is unhinged
Your platform is a mess
While a peaceful aura's above us
You're dripping with stress

It's time you examine
The threads which you wear
Not cast aspersions upon us
Try a breath of fresher air

This tide will not turn
There are millions of us
There won't be civil war
And impeachment's a bust

While you keep on sobbing
Crocodilian tears
We patiently envision
Seven more Trumpian years

Written by RayRay 8/22/17

Sheriff Joe

He gave him a pardon
And it drove the Left wild
Writing profusely
Supreme Court briefs to be filed

He dared to emancipate
This grandfatherly man
Who was doing his job
Near some sage brush and sand

Dressed them in pink slippers
Matched up with the chains
Fed them bread and some water
And In a tent they'd remain

Forget about GITMO
It was OK to let go
So the most brutal of criminals
Got traded back to their home

Presidential pardons
Are the price that you pay
Should you win your election
You can have it your way

We let Mr. Nixon
Walk away then
From Watergate leakage
With the stroke of a pen

They labeled Joe racist
When he stopped at the gate
Judging contempt
Making Illegal entry OK

So pick your fights wisely
It makes better sense
Imagine prosecuting your poppa
Because he was protecting a fence

Written by RayRay 8/28/17

Harvey

The rain hit so hard
With no place to go
A sea level town
Galvestonians know

Houston's a problem
A similar call
The tide it came in
60 inches in all

Devastation abounds
Masters and pets
Leveling homes
Drownings to death

Catastrophe reigns
Heeding the call
Yet duty remains
By helping them all

The President came
Melania too
While FEMA engaged
With water and food

The heart of a Texan
Always there on display
From El Paso to Dallas
They raise 'em that way

We pray for recovery
Let the waters recede
Rebuild their lives quickly
With laser like speed

Written by RayRay 8/30/17

Impeach This

So go right ahead
And give it a try
We're anxious to see
More Liberals cry

We saw the same tears
When Hillary caved
She slid down the tubes
Watched Democracy saved

So go right ahead
Knock yourself out
Spend precious time
Just flailing about

Every new day
You grow angry and tense
Dread seven more years
Of Donald and Pence

So go right ahead
And give it your all
Gather up your support
But prepare for the fall

You'll rely on amendments
And hope they will work
But it's gonna take more
Than naming a jerk

So go right ahead
And hire your best
Law firms with grudges
And hope they attest

Prepare for a battle
Like a snowflake in May
It will melt every time
No matter what you may pray

So go right ahead
Let the Congress impeach
It will collapse in the sand
Like the castle on the beach

It's time to face up
That impeachment's a fraud
Political Science will fail
When experiments are flawed

Written by RayRay 9/1/17

You Don't Tug on Superman's Cape©

The climate is boiling
Hurricanes are destroying
The Congress is annoying
Let's blame it on Trump

North Korea's provoking
Marijuana's been toking
Emissions are choking
So blame it on Trump

Woman are freaking
Abortions they're seeking
Fracking is leaking
It's gotta be Trump

Whites are depleted
Blacks are mistreated
Immigration impeded
It must be the Trump

Healthcare is fleeting
The Russians conceding
That Hillary's been cheating
The reason is Trump

The sun didn't shine
Poor grapes on the vine
While newspapers whine
It's all due to Trump

It must be his power
Leaping over Trump Tower
Clark Kent every hour
His Superman stunt

One man gets the credit
No one lets him forget it
That he wasn't vetted
The Nation's been stumped

So let's hit the piñata
Treat him as fodder
His sons and his daughter
Everyday they get dumped

So blame this one man
As much as you can
Just don't let them pass
A kryptonite ban

Written by RayRay 9/13/17
©Title credit to Jim Croce...RIP

Boy They Cried Wolf

The Left it appears
Keeps sounding alarms
Coding it red
Think they're doing us harm

Banging their drums
Leading a march
Making their noise
But our shirts still have starch

They started a riot
Rattled our ears
But you're clearly frustrated
About his 4 freaking years

The louder you yell
The less you are heard
It drones in our head
But it hardly disturbs

When you repeat and repeat
And the chorus persists
On deaf ears it falls
And the audience resists

You hope that your movement
Will change how we think
You demand our improvement
Infer we are freaks

Fascist supremacists
We hear it each day
Mysogynist homophobes
You won't let us lay

The boy who cried wolf
Misplayed many strong hands
He tried building sand castles
On the beach in the sand

You cry fire so often
We just can't conceive
When the real smoke is upon us
We just won't believe

Your strategy is failing
It just won't make sense
While 60 million deplorables
Will always come to his defense

Written by RayRay 9/7/17

The East Side Story

Up at the podium
As foe or as friend
He's on the East side
At the aging U N

They all sat dumbfounded
Not even a peep
In 30 odd languages
Translating his speech

All Heads of State
Headphones on their ears
Hearing him bury you
It just might appear

This man at the mic
Won't stop letting it go
No fear in his voice
Make sure that they know

The choices they make
He made it so clear
It's socialism they seek
Lands them flat on their rear

Who could have thunk it
Elton's words would forebode
Foresaw North Korea's dictator
A Rocket Man show

In front of all of those flags
So each country behold
Whether a Shark or a Jet
Len Bernstein's story's retold

Written by RayRay 9/21/17

Hit Me with Your Best Shot

Stick and stones
Which you have thrown
Fall far short
And is well known

Those laundry lists
Long and deep
Won't make a dent
In what you seek

The racist slurs
Have grown so lame
They're tired words
And become inane

The anger reeks
The temper smells
Rants and raves
Define yourselves

While we sit back
And absorb the blow
Rope a dope
Like an Ali show

The voting booths
Won the day
Silent strength
Dare I say

We raised a glass
Dug in our heels
Deflected stabs
You spun your wheels

But when you tire
From this long walk
Then at last
We all should talk

Find common ground
It does exist
You'll get much more
When arms don't twist

The more you yell
The less we hear
No one listens
In a noisy ear

If you persist
And drive the spike
8 years of thumbs
Will plug the dike

Written by RayRay 9/26/17

Player Protests

So you've been uninvited
To the President's home
You know it's up to the host
To have hospitality shown

You've earned the respect
Of your loyalest fans
They've spent hard earned money
So they could sit in the stands

Although it's your right
To raise up your fist
To show your displeasure
And peacefully resist

There are others that feel
A slap in the face
A cold hearted swell
A wave of disgrace

Most people know
Who work in this land
When you dis your employer
You'll see a red slip in hand

You've benefited greatly
Sharpened your skill
Earned opportunity
That very few will

The choice where you protest
Is what concerns those
Who honor this country
With flags and uniformed clothes

You want our respect
To hear what u say
Couldn't this be accomplished
After the game that you play?

Mutual respect
As much as we can
You give us your sport
Please honor your fan

It's as simple a trade-off
Don't you agree?
I respect you
And you respect me

Written by RayRay 9/24/17

Thick Matters

You think you can weaken us
Breaking our backs
Wrangling our fortitude
Then go for the sack

Your strategy's failing
For the whole world to see
Global and borderless
Well it just ain't for me

I do believe in culture
To learn from the rest
But stuffing our throat
Is failing our test

Just like an iceberg
Solid and free
90 percent of our mass
Lies under the sea

Roots that are deep
With values that last
Family and faith
We are up to the task

So go swing your bats
Tackle and block
We're thick as a wall
Made of concreted stock

You judge our intelligence
You think we're insane
Don't see it your way
Play the Burger King game

At the end of the day
Just don't count your chips
We will stay at the bridge table
And withstand all of your tricks

Written by RayRay 9/26/17

A Prayer for Las Vegas

They came for a concert
They came there to play
The best Strip show on Earth
Was Humanity on display

Hijacking trucks
To transport those hurt
Shielding your loved ones
Left your own blood in the dirt

Bullets rained down
From a hotel in the sky
With no place to run
And no place to hide

Brave and courageous
Were EMTs and police
Risking their lives
To get this sniper to cease

Nine minutes of terror
Bodies all lain
500 plus Americans
Left wounded or slain

We pray for their healing
We honor the dead
What happened in Vegas
Is mourning instead

Coming to grips with
These hateful details
But I'm placing my money
That LOVE will prevail

Your candlelight vigil
Brought us to our knees
Graceful and caring
For times just like these

The debates will continue
Answers will be sought
But blaming and naming
Will add up to naught

"Long Live Las Vegas"
This City of Sin
You showed the whole world
That you know how to win

Written by RayRay 10/4/17

What's Become of Us

Raw thoughts are spinning
Around in my head
Where is the outrage?
Are we emotionally dead?

Keep spinning the stories
Keep deflecting the truth
Death that means nothing
By God's grace it's not you

Your reaction's appalling
It's really not right
Carnage means nothing
As long as you're not in the sight

The snowflaking players
An insignificant mess
Let them kneel if they like
Because we could care less

Your focus is troubling
Completely off track
Free speech is your mantra
Gun laws to attack

While families are hurting
Their loved ones in pain
But all you can think of
Is showing disdain

It's chilling to see this
The death of your souls
So consumed by your hatred
That your gyroscope froze

Come to your senses
Smell something real
It's time you woke up
And started to feel

Your tiring old story
Oh give us a break
What the heck happened
For humanity's sake

Time to look in the mirror
Take time and pause
You're failing your brethren
For the sake of your cause

Written by RayRay 10/5/17

Let's Do the Twist

Her reaction was so pitiful
She just could not resist
To politicize the fallen
Cuss the notion to enlist

Only 1% of families
Can ever know the pain
To hear a knock upon the door
And announce his sacred name

They DO know what may lie in store
And accept that ultimate price
Gladly give their life for Country
Not to fuel a cruel device

Words of sorrow don't come easy
Mostly they fall flat
Most of us feel a tying tongue
When we try expressing that

Congress.. they may sign the check
That a soldier rarely sees
They're executing missions
Those funds for families

We owe them debts of gratitude
And not political gains
Can't we put our mouths aside
And honor his remains?

To twist a soldier's legacy
Like a butt upon cement
The meaning of that 60's song
Is not what Chubby Checker meant

Written by RayRay 10/19/17

"It's deja vu all over again." Yogi Berra

They say that Trump colluded
To steal the votes away
The Russian Bear intruded
Spoiling Hillary's glory day

The Cold War hasn't ended
It's heating up indeed
No different than the race to space
Perhaps Uranium increases speed

We paint them as the boogeymen
Just like on Halloween night
Wooden dolls are nesting
Must be the Trojan Horse inside

Some curse the name of Putin
But on the other hand
We're making deals behind closed doors
Assisting Mother Russia Land

They helped us on the Eastern Front
Squeezing Hitler's frozen troops
But a Communist's a dirty word
That's what we learned in school

It is a world community
So let's reach out with our hands
It's time to stop confusing us
About their insidious plans

I think of my descendants
Who grew up in the East
I still enjoy a Polish
Russian Vodka Kielbasa feast

Please put aside hysteria
In spite of what is said
Red is still a primary color
Not a place to dread

Written by RayRay 10/24/17

Jerusalem

290 miles long
9 to 80 miles wide
The sea to the West
Enemies on all sides

Israel's sovereignty
Always put the test
The world's eyes are upon them
A US Embassy move they detest

For 2000 years
The world would reject
To consider Jerusalem
A capital to respect

So enter our President
So new on the job
Shaking up history
Making them sob

Who stands for Israel?
Raise up your hand
Built from the ashes
Of a desert like sand

Make no mistake
Condemn what you feel
Let's move from Berlin to Hamburg
Be attacked with the same zeal

We committed in Congress
To move 60 miles East
But hid behind waivers
With Presidents so weak

The people rejoice
Let the opposition rage
I'm applauding our President
For turning the page

For 5,000 years
The Jews get displaced
Holocaust in the 40's
In '48 given their space

The world is alarmed
That peace is at risk
Move to a new building
They just couldn't resist

So burn up some flags
Of the Red White and Blue
But to the Israelis
This ain't anything new

Written by RayRay 12/7/17

The Plot Thickens

Agatha Christie
Is astir in her grave
Watching from heaven
How politicians behave

Causing each side
Enduring distress
Wishing they had minicams
On the D.C. Orient Express

Peering inside
Of Mueller's war room
Laden with operatives
Putting Trump in their zoom

Discovering iPhones
With dubious texts
Demoting attorneys
God knows who will be next

Conspiracy theories
Who dunnits abound
No one trusts no one
While Miss Marple's around

Confusing the public
As to whom is to blame
Clues that confound us
May drive us insane

Department of Justice
Plus the F B of I
Intelligence committees
All questioning why

One side's determined
To bring down the King
While the other side hunkers
Their heels in the West Wing

It feels like a movie
In front of our eyes
With an ending I'm betting
Will be a clueless surprise

Written by RayRay 12/8/17

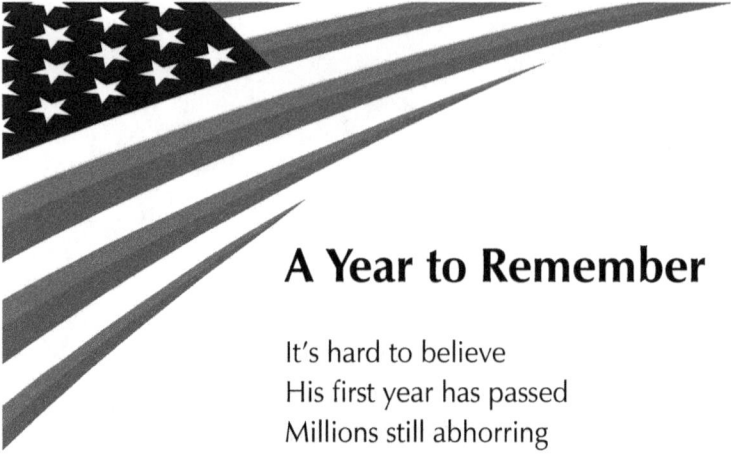

A Year to Remember

It's hard to believe
His first year has passed
Millions still abhorring
How the ballots were cast

Still shaking their heads
They still can't conceive
They're afraid to imagine
What lies up his sleeve

The pundits were stumped
While Hollywood wailed
Madonna's in Portugal
Her records have flailed

Gorsuch confirmed
Sessions was named
Mad dog promoted
Conservatives reign

NOKO is arming
Strutting their stuff
Sometimes you lose
When called on your bluff

The Eclipse casted a shadow
Harvey blew through
Puerto Rico got leveled
And they blame it on you

The Wall's still an issue
Tax code being reviewed
Healthcare is sickly
The Left feeling blue

Players are kneeling
Ignoring the flag
Hailing freedom of speech
Either way it's so sad

Antifa is ready
As Anonymous states
Leftists scream towards the heavens
From a nightmare awake

What lies ahead
We can only surmise
But for many Americans
Tensions surely will rise

So it's on to year 2
Let's be hopeful at least
We pray that the sun
Will still rise in the East

Written by RayRay 12/9/17

The second year of *The Trump Chronicle*
is already underway

www.ingramcontent.com/pod-product-compliance
Lightning Source LLC
Chambersburg PA
CBHW071059090426
42737CB00013B/2392